P9-DGV-571

Looking at Literature Through Primary Sources™

Uncle Tom's Cabin and the Abolitionist Movement

Julie Carlson

rosen central

Primary Source™

The Rosen Publishing Group, Inc., New York

Published in 2004 by The Rosen Publishing Group, Inc.
29 East 21st Street, New York, NY 10010

Unless otherwise attributed, all quotes in this book are excerpted from *Uncle Tom's Cabin*.

Library of Congress Cataloging-in-Publication Data

Carlson, Julie, 1980–
Uncle Tom's cabin and the abolitionist movement/by Julie Carlson.— 1st ed.
    p. cm. — (Looking at literature through primary sources)
Summary: Traces the process and influences behind the writing of Harriet Beecher Stowe's novel, *Uncle Tom's Cabin*, which was published when the nation was torn over the issue of slavery and headed toward Civil War.
Includes bibliographical references and index.
ISBN 0-8239-4508-1 (library binding)
1. Stowe, Harriet Beecher, 1811–1896. *Uncle Tom's Cabin*. 2. Antislavery movements— United States—History—19th century. 3. Didactic fiction, American—History and criticism. 4. Antislavery movements in literature. 5. Southern States—In literature. 6. Uncle Tom (Fictitious character) 7. African Americans in literature. 8. Slavery in literature. 9. Race in literature. [1. Stowe, Harriet Beecher, 1811–1896. *Uncle Tom's Cabin*. 2. American literature—History and criticism. 3. Antislavery movements. 4. African Americans in literature. 5. Slavery in literature. 6. Race in literature.]
I. Title. II. Series.
PS2954.U6C37 2004
813'.3—dc22

                                                                    2003015889

Manufactured in the United States of America

On the cover: An 1853 portrait of Harriet Beecher Stowe *(top)*; a woodcut image of a slave in chains that was often used in abolitionist publications *(bottom left)*; and the cover of the first edition of *Uncle Tom's Cabin*.

CONTENTS

INTRODUCTION

In times of conflict, people search for ways to be heard. Literature and other artistic expressions have often had as much of an impact influencing change as have political and scientific debates. One outstanding example of this is Harriet Beecher Stowe's novel *Uncle Tom's Cabin*. Published in 1852, *Uncle Tom's Cabin* demonstrates the influence a writer may have in times of social change.

Uncle Tom's Cabin serves as an excellent example of how many American women of the mid-1800s reacted to slavery. We can see what drew women to reform movements during that time. The success of *Uncle Tom's Cabin* was an important marker in the recognition of women as writers and activists.

The book garnered renewed attention in the United States during the civil rights movement of the 1960s. Until then, there had been little reaction to the racial stereotypes Stowe had used in *Uncle Tom's Cabin*. But black rights leaders of the twentieth century began to criticize how she represented blacks in the novel.

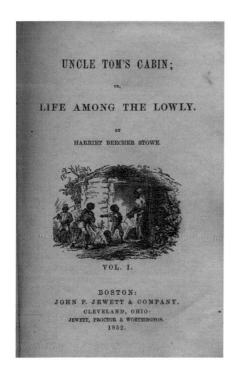

UNCLE TOM'S CABIN;

or,

LIFE AMONG THE LOWLY.

BY

HARRIET BEECHER STOWE.

VOL. I.

BOSTON:
JOHN P. JEWETT & COMPANY.
CLEVELAND, OHIO:
JEWETT, PROCTOR & WORTHINGTON.
1852.

♦♦♦ **This is the title page from the first edition of *Uncle Tom's Cabin*, bearing the book's often overlooked subtitle *or, Life Among the Lowly*. Stowe's antislavery novel was so widely read during the 1850s that it generated international sympathy for African American slaves. Nevertheless, its characters helped to spread stereotypes about African Americans.**

Stowe praises Uncle Tom in the novel for being submissive, passing this off as a "black virtue." In the 1960s, "Uncle Tom" became a derogatory term used to describe blacks who tried too hard to cooperate with the demands of white people.

Uncle Tom's Cabin established the genre of the protest novel. Stowe proved that fiction could effectively persuade people to unite for a cause. Back in 1852, Harriet Beecher Stowe demonstrated that a novel could be used as an essential tool to change the minds of society's great thinkers and leaders. The novel continues to be a subject of controversy and a source of admiration for each new generation that encounters it. As a result of the huge success of *Uncle Tom's Cabin*, writers today often meld fact and fiction to make a political statement.

Chapter 1

Early Theories of Race in America

As leaders from the original thirteen colonies discussed ways to join together, slavery became a highly charged issue. The Declaration of Independence, drafted in 1776 by Thomas Jefferson, defined the "natural rights of Americans." General George Washington, commander of the American army, owned slaves. So did Thomas Jefferson. With the formation of the United States, only white men gained liberty.

Delegates at the Constitution Convention in 1789 who were against slavery had to make a tough decision. They were convinced that the colonies could survive only by joining together under one flag. But they also knew that the wealthy, powerful planters from the South would not accept an end to slavery. For the sake of the new country, many signers agreed not to outlaw slavery in the Constitution.

Common Ideas About Race

While white southern men reaped the benefits of slave labor, people on both sides of the slavery issue based their arguments

At top, a painting depicts George Washington watching over a group of slaves on his estate in Mount Vernon, New York; at bottom is an 1845 portrait of Isaac Jefferson, who was one of Thomas Jefferson's slaves.

on assumptions about race. Most white Americans during that time believed that the negative, condescending stereotypes of black people were true.

People create stereotypes when they assign specific traits to an entire group of people. In the American colonies, most whites had decided that blacks were less intelligent and civilized than whites. Some whites even alleged that black people could not feel pain or experience love the way that whites did.

Theories of Racial Origins

Scientists tried to explain differences between races and how they stood apart from each other. Early popular scientific theories encouraged people to think in generalizations.

Monogenesis and Polygenesis

Between the eighteenth and nineteenth centuries, there were two main theories of racial origin. The first was called monogenesis, which means "one beginning." Supporters of monogenesis believed that there was one original race of humans who spread to different continents. Life in new environments caused people to change physically and mentally.

Scientists (who were white) said that whites were the first race. According to them, the other races developed from the degeneration, or worsening, of the white race. In the nineteenth century, this idea gradually gave way to a new premise.

The second theory, called polygenesis, or "many beginnings," suggested that races sprung up around the earth about the same time. The differences between each race existed from the beginning of human life. Some scientists believed that the races were permanently separate and unequal.

Although these theories of racial origin were drastically different, whites smugly accepted the theory that they were permanently superior. White people used these racial theories to justify slavery. If black people really were inferior, as whites thought, then it made sense to treat them differently.

Alexander Kinmont's Theories of Race

Harriet Beecher Stowe's views on race were influenced by a series of lectures she attended in Cincinnati during the winter of 1837 to 1838. The lecturer was a teacher, Alexander Kinmont. With arguments based on religion, not science, Kinmont proposed that God had put each race of people on the earth with a particular mission. Kinmont regarded blacks as naturally cheerful, submissive, patient, hard-working, and spiritual. Whites, he declared, were more intelligent, civilized, and ambitious.

Kinmont also perceived white people to be dangerous. The white man's desire for power and success, according to Kinmont, often led him to act with greed and rage. In Kinmont's mind, blacks embodied the gentler virtues of love, forgiveness, and attachment to family and home. These values correspond to traditional Christian values. Because blacks exhibited these

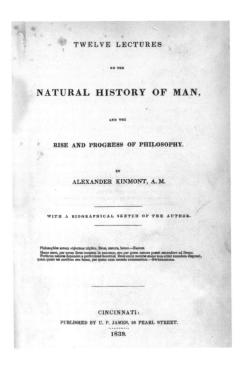

◆◆◆ **This is the title page of Alexander Kinmont's** *Twelve Lectures on the Natural History of Man, and the Rise and Progress of Philosophy.* **Published in 1839, a year after Kinmont's death, the book gathers some of the lecturer's most important theories on race. Like other opponents of slavery of his era, Kinmont stereotyped blacks even as he spoke favorably of them.**

"natural" virtues, Kinmont was convinced that their destiny was greater than whites.

To Kinmont, slavery was evil because it took advantage of what he considered the black race's childlike ignorance and eagerness to please. He compared so-called black attributes with Christian values and insisted that they should be celebrated, not exploited.

Slaves as Ideal Christians

Although she never offered a detailed statement of her beliefs, Harriet Beecher Stowe imagined that blacks experienced religion more deeply than whites. The black slave seemed like an ideal Christian to her. Stowe believed that forced to live in degrading conditions, the slave obeyed and forgave his master. The pious character of Tom in *Uncle Tom's Cabin* demonstrates Stowe's idea that black people embodied the spirit of Christianity. In the following passage, she describes a religious meeting in which Tom leads the other slaves in prayer.

> **Nothing could exceed the touching simplicity, the child-like earnestness, of his prayer, enriched with the language of Scripture, which seemed so entirely to have wrought itself into his being, as to have become a part of himself.**

Kinmont's and Stowe's stereotype of the black person may have seemed almost favorable to blacks in 1850. It was apparently considered radical. A visitor to a plantation in the South was almost certain to find mild-mannered, religious, obedient slaves. In Stowe's words, "the negro mind, impassioned and imaginative, always attaches itself to hymns and expressions of a vivid and pictorial nature."

Kinmont and Stowe assumed that black people were born with certain attributes and behaviors. Neither actively questioned why the slaves they observed appeared to behave in certain ways.

There were few ways for colonial slaves to exhibit "intelligence" as it was measured by whites. According to African American scholar Henry Louis Gates Jr. in a 1997 interview, after the 1739 Stoner Rebellion in South Carolina—one of the first violent slave rebellions in the United States—southern states began to pass laws aimed at eliminating the possibility of future revolts by

Chapter 2

The Issue of Slavery in Nineteenth-Century America

In the decades leading up to the U.S. Civil War, a rift developed between the North and South. Although many factors contributed to the division, at the center of the conflict was the issue of slavery. Southern planters depended on the labor of slaves.

The Missouri Compromise

In 1820, Missouri wanted to become a state. At that time, there were an equal number of free states and slave states. This meant that the North and South were equally represented in the U.S. Senate. Senators from the North and South fought over whether to admit Missouri as a slave state or a free state. Eventually, they agreed to admit Missouri as a slave state and allow Maine, which was then a part of Massachusetts, to become its own free state.

Congress created a boundary across the middle of the country as it then existed. New states south of the line would be admitted to the Union as slave states. New states north of the

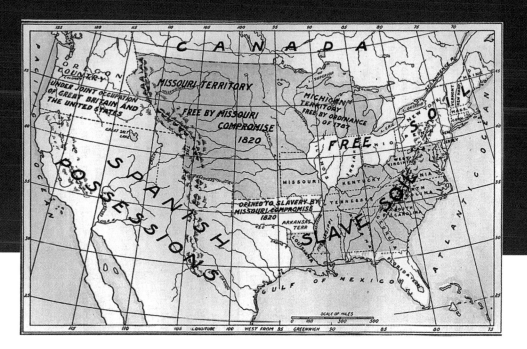

This map shows the division of American land between free states and territories and slave states and territories as a result of the Missouri Compromise of 1820.

line would be admitted as free states. This decision was called the Missouri Compromise. But as more states entered the Union, problems continued to arise. Many southern states talked about seceding, or breaking away, from the Union.

Abolitionists, people who wanted to see slavery end, traveled south to report on plantation conditions. Several former slaves gave accounts of their lives in the South. One was Frederick Douglass, a freed slave who published his autobiography. People started to speak up about their concerns. An antislavery movement was building.

THE FUGITIVE SLAVE LAW.

◆◆◆ This broadside, printed by S. M. Africanus in 1850 in Hartford, Connecticut, bears the text of the Fugitive Slave Act, which was passed that year. Africanus also included his objections to the law and an appeal to citizens not to comply with it.

The Fugitive Slave Act of 1850

The passing of the Fugitive Slave Act of 1850 increased the tension between the North and the South. The act mandated that anyone who apprehended a runaway slave, in a free or slave state, was required to return the slave to the owner. The punishment for assisting fugitives was a fine of up to $1,000 or six months in prison. This law did not require the presence of a judge or jury to decide if a captured person actually was a fugitive slave.

The government paid federal officers for every runaway slave they returned to the owner. To establish ownership, a slaveholder needed only to swear that a black person was his escaped slave. Freed blacks were in danger of being captured as much as actual runaway slaves. The Fugitive Slave Act made slave catching a profitable business, and it forced citizens of free states to comply with the demands of slaveholders. The act angered many northern citizens who did not want to be involved in the upkeep of slavery.

Harriet Beecher Stowe was particularly outraged by the new law, which contradicted values she thought the government should uphold. Near the beginning of *Uncle Tom's Cabin*, Senator Bird explains the law to his wife. Her response is probably similar to what Stowe's would have been.

> "And what is the law? It don't forbid us to shelter these poor creatures a night, does it, and to give 'em something comfortable to eat, and a few clothes, and send them quietly about their business? . . . Now, John, I want to know if you think such a law as that is right and Christian?"

The senator argues with her, insisting that in times of public agitation, Americans must put aside their personal feelings. Mrs. Bird counters, "Obeying God never brings on public evils. I know it can't. It's always safest, all round, to do as He bids us." That night, the runaway slave Eliza arrives at the Birds' residence, and Senator Bird, in spite of his political opinions, is compelled to help her.

What angered Stowe even more about the Fugitive Slave Act were the Christian leaders who did not speak out against the new legislation. So, Stowe resolved to write her book against slavery.

A Variety of Approaches to Abolition

In the 1800s, many northerners focused their energies on abolition, or the elimination of slavery in the United States. Other abolitionists did not want to change laws about slavery in the South. They wanted to change the ways that southerners thought about slavery by setting an example.

American Colonization Society

Many Americans had objected to slavery since the Revolutionary War. But few of them offered clear solutions to the problem. In 1817, some well-known politicians founded the American Colonization Society. The group's purpose was to raise money to buy slaves from the South and send them to Africa. Once there, they believed, emancipated blacks could build their own colony with the guidance of white Americans. Free blacks in the North had worked hard to be accepted as Americans and didn't want to leave for Africa. But the response to colonization caused more discussion, and the antislavery movement gained momentum.

The American Anti-Slavery Society

In 1831, a Boston journalist named William Lloyd Garrison began to publish the *Liberator*, an outspoken antislavery newspaper. Its first readers and subscribers were free blacks living in the North. In 1833, Garrison joined forces with Arthur Tappan, a wealthy man from New York who had started an abolitionist group. Together, the two men formed the American Anti-Slavery Society (AASS). For several years, the AASS organized rallies and revivals and held discussions about slavery.

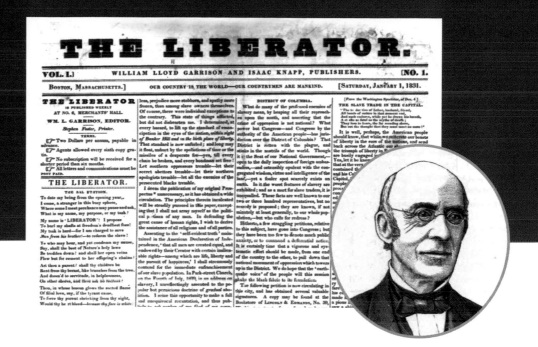

This is the front page from the January 1, 1831, edition of the *Liberator*. Between 1831 and 1865, William Lloyd Garrison *(inset)* used the *Liberator* to spread his militant antislavery views. He consistently called for immediate abolition and often referred to slave-owning as a crime. Many Southern states outlawed the paper and called for Garrison's prosecution.

There were problems within the AASS, though. In 1840, the society split into several organizations. Tappan's group was the American and Foreign Anti-Slavery Society, which did not allow female members to vote. Garrison's group supported women activists and further reforms in American society. His group aimed to change public opinion in order to end slavery. James Birney formed the Liberty Party, which worked through the political system to effect changes, rather than appeal to the public.

Lyman Beecher and Lane Theological Seminary

In Cincinnati, Ohio, Lane Theological Seminary became the setting for some heated and highly publicized discussions about slavery. Lyman Beecher, the father of Harriet Beecher Stowe, was president of the school. Beecher supported colonization in Africa as a solution to slavery. In 1834, Theodore Weld, a student, arrived at Lane Seminary. Weld roused his classmates to challenge many of the conservative religious teachings of President Beecher. The students formed two different antislavery groups on campus and incited a series of fiery debates about colonization. A significant number of them left Lane Seminary and enrolled at Oberlin College, a more liberal institution. The incident was a blow to the school and to Lyman Beecher. By 1845, there were no students left at Lane.

While all these groups challenged slavery publicly, one of the most important efforts against slavery went on in secret.

The Underground Railroad

The Underground Railroad was a network of people who helped guide and protect runaway slaves as they traveled to freedom in northern states or Canada. Quakers had been doing this since the 1780s. By the 1830s, the Underground Railroad had become more active. The Fugitive Slave Act made transportation of slaves even more dangerous. Many brave men and women put themselves at risk to help slaves reach freedom.

Illustrations of the American Anti-Slavery Almanac for 1840.

"Our Peculiar Domestic Institutions."

Northern Hospitality—New-York nine months law. [The Slave steps out of the Slave State, and his chains fall. A Free State, with another chain, stands ready to re-enslave him.]

Burning of McIntosh at St. Louis, in April, 1836.

Shewing how slavery improves the condition of the female sex.

The Negro Pew, or "Free" Seats for black Christians.

Mayor of New-York refusing a Cartman's license to a colored Man.

Servility of the Northern States in arresting and returning fugitive Slaves.

Selling a Mother from her Child.

Hunting Slaves with dogs and guns. A Slave drowned by the dogs.

"Poor things, 'they can't take care of themselves.'"

Mothers with young Children at work in the field.

A Woman chained to a Girl, and a Man in irons at work in the field.

Branding Slaves.

Cutting up a Slave in Kentucky.

Paid.　　Unpaid.

This broadside, published by the American Anti-Slavery Society, is a collection of illustrations used in the society's 1840 almanac, which focused on the cruelties of slavery. Each year, the AASS distributed an almanac containing a variety of abolitionist materials including poems, drawings, and essays.

Women in the Abolitionist Movement

Female abolitionists had difficulty being recognized by men in the abolitionist movement. A major reason for the breakup of the American Anti-Slavery Society was that the members disagreed on the role of women, who were excluded from the World Anti-Slavery Convention in 1840. In 1848, female activists organized the Seneca Falls Convention. Women met to declare the equality of men and women. Women's rights and abolition went hand in hand.

During the writing of *Uncle Tom's Cabin*, Stowe corresponded with other women abolitionist writers. They encouraged each other and reported on the latest developments. There was a collective spirit among the women behind the anti-slavery movement. The theme of women helping women is also prevalent in *Uncle Tom's Cabin*.

Arguments Against Abolition

Most pro-slavery arguments were based on the contention that blacks were not really people. In *Uncle Tom's Cabin*, Stowe shows how a slave owner enjoys treating a very young slave as if he were an animal.

> "Hulloa, Jim Crow!" said Mr. Shelby, whistling, and snapping a bunch of raisins towards him, "pick that up, now!" The child scampered, with all his little strength, after the prize, while his master laughed.

This is the front page of the June 20, 1850, edition of the *North Star,* the abolitionist newspaper published by Frederick Douglass *(inset)* between 1847 and 1863. In addition to advocating universal emancipation, Douglass used the paper to call for women's rights.

In 1853, Josiah Priest wrote *Bible Defence of Slavery,* suggesting that Africans did not feel pain when beaten, did not have the same connections to family as whites, and were not human according to the Bible. Whether or not slave owners agreed with this thinking, they were primarily afraid of what would happen to their economy if slavery were revoked.

Abolitionists were often attacked, and antislavery printing presses were burned. Some abolitionists were even killed by angry mobs. Long before the Civil War broke out in 1861, the fight against slavery had become dangerous.

Chapter 3

Harriet Beecher Stowe

arriet Beecher was born on June 14, 1811, in Litchfield, Connecticut, the seventh of thirteen children. Her father, Lyman Beecher, was the minister of a well-known Calvinist church. Her mother, Roxana Foote Beecher, was an intelligent and educated woman, with interests in science and poetry. She died in 1816, when Harriet was only four years old. Roxana's influence on Harriet and her sisters lasted throughout their adult lives. This is reflected in *Uncle Tom's Cabin* by the character of Augustine St. Clare, whose own mother "had been a woman of uncommon elevation and purity of character." He, too, views his mother as an example of heavenly grace. He says of her that "she was divine! . . . there was no trace of any human weakness or error about her," and he claims that she "was a direct embodiment and personification of the New Testament

A year after Roxana's death, Lyman married Harriet Porter. The children described her as a kind woman who was strict and refined.

Lyman educated his children about philosophy and religion. It was mostly his seven sons who benefited from these lessons.

This photograph of the Beecher family was taken in 1855. Front row, from left to right: Isabella, Catharine, Lyman (Harriet's father), Mary, and Harriet. Second row, from left to right: Thomas, William, Edward, Charles, and Henry Ward. James Beecher, another of Harriet's brothers, is shown in the inset at bottom left.

Indeed, Harriet's father had often lamented that she was a girl and not a boy. He felt that her intelligence was wasted because women did not have a place in academic circles.

Lyman Beecher's religious teachings were traditional and conservative. He strongly disapproved of modern religious groups, especially the Unitarians, and spoke in favor of the old church of New England. The Bible was the basis of his theology, and he would not compromise. In Lyman's eyes, if it was written in the Bible, it was not to be contested.

Harriet's Siblings

All seven of Harriet's surviving brothers (an eighth brother died as a child) became ministers like their father, who exerted enormous pressure on them to work in the church. But Harriet's brothers James and George eventually committed suicide. James had worked as the captain of a clipper ship but knew he would become a minister eventually. "Father will pray me into it," he said. Charles resisted for a long time before he too joined the others in the church. Settled in New Orleans, he taught music and worked as a cotton clerk. Through this job, Charles supplied Harriet with much of the information she used to write *Uncle Tom's Cabin*.

Of the three of Harriet's four sisters who survived into adulthood, Mary was the only one who chose a domestic life. Catharine worked on reforms for women, particularly in education (although she opposed women's right to vote). Isabella was a passionate advocate of women's suffrage and abolition. Eccentric, some of her quirks caused people to think she was insane. Although she possibly suffered from mental illness, her enthusiasm for her causes had a profound effect on Harriet.

Hartford Female Seminary

In 1823, Catharine Beecher founded Hartford Female Seminary, a Christian school for young women. In addition to completing her

◆◆◆ At the time when Harriet Beecher attended the Hartford Female Seminary, it was one of few schools that took the education of girls seriously. This is an etching of the school as it appeared around 1862.

own studies there, Harriet, by age thirteen, was instructing slightly younger girls. She began writing poetry and myths in her spare time, but Catharine disapproved and found Harriet a tutor to occupy her with more "useful" activities.

Harriet's Conversion

During her time at the seminary, Harriet experienced a religious conversion. At age fourteen, she told her father that she had accepted Jesus Christ as her savior. He instructed her to look deeper into her heart and make sure she really was saved. It was not just the Beecher boys who suffered from their father's unrelenting religious piety. Fear and guilt about the quality of her religious faith haunted Harriet into adulthood.

◆◆◆ This photograph of Harriet Beecher Stowe and her husband, Calvin, was taken around 1850. Calvin, who encouraged Harriet in her writing career, also found success as an author. His *Origin and History of the Books of the Bible*, published in 1867, sold very well.

Harriet Begins to Write

In 1832, Harriet moved to Cincinnati with her family. There she joined a secret club, called the Semi Colon Club, with her sister Catharine. The women in this club read poetry, listened to music, and wrote compositions. With such a supportive group of friends, Harriet was encouraged to develop as a writer.

In Cincinnati, Harriet met Calvin Stowe, a widowed teacher at Lane Seminary. They married in January 1836.

Harriet soon gave birth to twin girls. In 1838, their son Henry was born. Harriet struggled to keep up with her responsibilities as a mother while Calvin worked at Lane Seminary. The school was losing money, so to make up for extra house expenses, Harriet wrote essays for various publications. She had another son, Frederick, in 1840.

The stress of being a housewife overwhelmed Harriet. She wanted to be a literary woman, and she often escaped her family obligations by writing stories. Calvin supported Harriet's endeavors, as did her sister Catharine, who found a publisher for her work. In 1843, *The May Flower*, a book of Harriet's short stories, was published.

That year, Harriet's brother George shot and killed himself. The incident devastated Harriet. A few months later, her third daughter Georgiana was born. She was a weak and sickly baby who required constant care. Calvin was traveling all the time, and Harriet was anxious and overworked. She became very ill. Catharine put together enough money to send Harriet to Vermont in 1846 to undergo the famous water cure. The water cure involved waking up each morning at 4 AM to be wrapped in thick woolen blankets. When the patient had perspired enough to soak the blankets, he or she was dipped into a cold bath. Harriet remained there for fifteen months, recovering from exhaustion.

In 1848, after Harriet returned to Cincinnati, she gave birth to a sixth child named Samuel Charles. Calvin went to Vermont six months later to try the water cure, leaving Harriet with little money. She began teaching a small group of children, including ex-slaves.

In 1849, Samuel Charles died in an outbreak of cholera. This hit Harriet harder than any other sorrow she had experienced. The pain stayed with her through the rest of her life. In *Uncle*

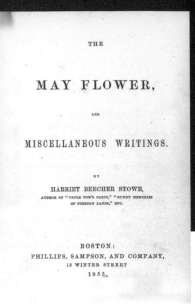

Harriet Beecher Stowe's *The May Flower*, first published in 1843, is a collection of stories about the descendants of the Pilgrims, who traveled from England to Massachusetts aboard the *Mayflower* in the seventeenth century. Above are the title pages from an 1855 printing of the book.

Tom's Cabin, many characters suffer the same kind of loss, and it was a point that many readers related to personally.

> St. Clare . . . laid his hand on Tom's, and bowed down his forehead on it.
>
> "O, Tom, my boy, the whole world is as empty as an egg-shell."
>
> "I know it, Mas'r, —I know it," said Tom; "but, oh, if Mas'r could only look up, —up where our dear Miss Eva is, —up to the dear Lord Jesus!"

Harriet Voices Her Opinion

In 1850, Bowdoin College in Brunswick, Maine, offered Calvin Stowe a teaching job. The family moved to Maine. That year, the last of their children, Charles, was born.

Harriet's sister Isabella wrote to her about the Fugitive Slave Act, which they both despised, and encouraged Harriet to voice her opinion. Harriet began to work on *Uncle Tom's Cabin*.

The Challenges of Being a Woman Writer

When Harriet Beecher Stowe wrote *Uncle Tom's Cabin*, women were not yet welcome in the literary world. One frustration that faced successful women of the time was that they were discouraged from acknowledging their own accomplishments. The only sense of pride a woman was entitled to show was that of her abilities as a mother. This prejudice did not stop some women from writing, but the works of female authors were rarely taken seriously.

Uncle Tom's Cabin received an extraordinary amount of attention from all over the world, especially for a novel written by a woman. Women writers of her time almost always wrote under assumed names, but Stowe wrote as herself. She expressed strong opinions about a sensitive subject, and there was a risk involved in attaching her name to it. Most women writers of the time published tame stories about keeping house and raising children. Stowe tackled a controversial issue that attracted a lot of public interest. Her use of regional dialect instead of rigid prose was also highly unusual in a woman's writing. Of course, the most radical element of *Uncle Tom's Cabin* was its cast of sympathetic black characters.

Rejecting the Idea of Equality

It may appear that Stowe had revolutionary ideas about the place of a woman in the world. After all, she broke several rules upheld by her society just by writing a novel. But Stowe and her sister Catharine worked to enhance the power of women within the home. Motherhood, in their opinion, required education and training like any other profession.

The sisters also shared a belief that women had a higher moral sense than men. The duty of women, they concluded, was to encourage their husbands to cultivate a better sense of right and wrong. Stowe judged the differences between men and women much how she differentiated between blacks and whites. That she rejected the idea of equality between the races or the sexes distinguished Stowe from women activists who struggled to gain voting privileges and the right to own property.

Not Quite an Abolitionist

Not all Americans who were antislavery were abolitionists. Abolitionists wanted slavery to end in the South—immediately, and by whatever means necessary. People like Stowe objected to the evils of slavery but did not believe that it could or should be forcibly terminated. Stowe wanted slaveholders to recognize their wrongdoings and free their slaves. Although she was outspoken

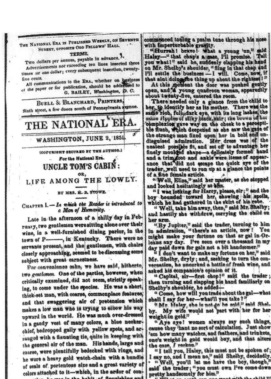

◆◆◆ Although the *National Era* was an abolitionist newspaper, it also published materials that were not related to the issue of slavery. The paper served also as a forum for literary ideas and to broadcast local and international news. This issue, released on June 2, 1851, included the first chapter of *Uncle Tom's Cabin.* Harriet Beecher Stowe's novel was published in the *National Era* as a series before it was published in book form.

about her moral opposition to slavery, she did not think it was her responsibility to bring about social change.

In her essay "Appeal to the Women of the Free States," in 1854, Stowe wrote, "The question is not, shall the wrongs of slavery exist, as they have, on their own territories? But shall we permit them to be extended over all the free territories of the United States?"

Stowe was concerned with slavery's evils spreading to free soil. Before writing *Uncle Tom's Cabin*, she had published work in the *National Era*, an antislavery paper. She had also written stories for a variety of magazines to earn money. But the success of *Uncle Tom's Cabin* was something she had never expected.

Chapter 4

Uncle Tom's Cabin

Many abolitionists wrote essays and lectured about the evils of slavery, but none of their works were as influential as *Uncle Tom's Cabin*. It was published first as a series in the *National Era* from June 1851 through April 1852. Readers responded positively to the series, and a small publishing company agreed to print it as a book in 1852. Few could imagine the success it would enjoy or the controversy it would create.

The Story

As the novel begins, readers meet the Shelbys, a couple who own slaves in Kentucky. They owe money to a slave trader named Haley and must sell two of their slaves to him to pay off the debt. The two chosen for sale are middle-aged Uncle Tom and Harry, a toddler. Harry's mother, Eliza, who is Mrs. Shelby's maid, is fiercely protective of her son. Two of her babies have died, and she will not let Harry be taken from her. She runs away with Harry in the middle of the night. Tom's wife, Chloe, urges him to escape with Eliza, but he won't. Tom, who has lived and worked on the plantation since Mr. Shelby was a baby, understands his "duty" as a slave. He goes willingly, but it breaks his heart to leave behind his wife and children.

Eliza makes a dangerous journey to the Ohio River and crosses into Ohio. Several people help her on her way north. Her husband, George Harris, from another plantation, has also escaped, and he and Eliza join each other at a Quaker settlement. Followed closely by the slave catchers, the Harris family flees to Sandusky, Ohio, where they can catch a ferry into Canada.

Tom meets a young white girl named Eva on a ship traveling down the river to the Deep South. Eva is an angelic, beautiful child who seems too good to be real. Eva takes a liking to Tom immediately. When she falls overboard and nearly drowns, Tom saves her. Eva's father, Augustine St. Clare, then agrees to buy Tom.

The St. Clare's estate is chaotic and lazy compared to the Shelbys'. Augustine is a good-hearted man, but his wife, Marie, is selfish and irritable. She always claims to be sick and complains about the slaves constantly. Another member of the household is Ophelia, Augustine's cousin from Vermont.

Ophelia opposes slavery but does not like the company of black people. Augustine buys her a slave girl named Topsy to test Ophelia's theories about education. Topsy has problems with discipline and cannot tell right from wrong. Ophelia almost gives up on teaching her, but Eva connects with her by being loving. Topsy has never been loved before. When she sees the effect of kindness on Topsy, Ophelia promises to try to love her.

Eva and Tom talk a lot about God and the Bible. Eva becomes ill and slowly dies. Her loving example changes the people around her. She asks her father to free Tom, but he is killed in a bar fight before he is able to do so. Marie St. Clare sells Tom again.

His new owner is Simon Legree, who could be said to represent the devil. He is violent and evil. He maintains his power over the slaves by pitting them against each other. Cassy, Legree's mistress, befriends Tom but does not share his love of God.

Cassy plans an escape with Legree's other mistress, Emmeline. They hide in the attic of the house, which Legree thinks is haunted. When Tom refuses to tell Legree where they have gone, Legree brutally beats him. George Shelby arrives at the plantation to save Tom, but it is too late. Tom dies, and George Shelby buries him. He swears on Tom's grave that he will do his part to end slavery.

On Shelby's return to Kentucky, he meets a woman from France named Madame de Thoux. They discover that she is George Harris's sister. Cassy is also on the boat, and it turns out that she is Eliza's mother. Madame de Thoux, Cassy, and

This engraving depicts a group of slaves escaping to freedom along the Underground Railroad. The Underground Railroad was not a precise trail but a vast network of paths, roads, and buildings that runaway slaves, with the help of abolitionists, followed to northern states and Canada.

Emmeline go to Montreal and meet George and Eliza, who are living there with Harry and a new baby girl. The family moves to France, George attends university, and they go on to Africa. George believes that is where he can do the most good for his people. George Shelby goes home and frees his slaves.

Inspirations for the Story

For eighteen years, Harriet Beecher Stowe lived in Cincinnati, across the Ohio River from Kentucky. During this time, Stowe had a lot of contact with freed blacks who told her about their lives as slaves in the South.

Visiting a Plantation

In the summer of 1833, Stowe visited an estate in Kentucky, where she witnessed the workings of a southern plantation. Although she did not interact very much with the slaves, Stowe remembered what she saw. Her friend Mary Dutton, who had joined her on that trip, later commented that many scenes in *Uncle Tom's Cabin* were reconstructed from their visit to Kentucky.

An Authentic Experience

During the novel, Eliza escapes to freedom. Her escape is based on the story of a real woman. In 1839, Stowe learned that one of her hired servants was a fugitive slave whose master was searching for her. Late one night, Stowe's husband and younger brother took the woman to a friend's home in the country where she could hide. That event is depicted in *Uncle Tom's Cabin* when Senator Bird transports Eliza to a safe house.

Creating Uncle Tom

Readers have tried to identify real people used by Stowe as models for her characters. Of special interest is Uncle Tom, who seems to be built out of Stowe's stereotype of the good Christian

EVA DRESSING UNCLE TOM.

Josiah Henson

At left, an illustrated page from *Uncle Tom's Cabin* depicting Eva and Tom; and at right, a portrait of Josiah Henson, after whom Harriet Beecher Stowe possibly modeled Uncle Tom. Stowe wrote the introduction for the 1858 reprint of Henson's autobiography, *Truth Stranger Than Fiction: Father Henson's Story of His Own Life.*

black man. One possible prototype for his character was Josiah Henson. After escaping enslavement, Henson became a clergyman in Canada and wrote an autobiography that supposedly inspired Stowe, who had read many abolitionist books, pamphlets, and slave narratives, including Josiah Henson's.

Another possible inspiration was the slave husband of one of Stowe's black servants. He had been sold to someone in the Deep South and had to leave behind his family, just like Uncle Tom.

Chapter 5

Stowe's Purpose in Writing *Uncle Tom's Cabin*

Stowe chose to present her political ideas in a fictional story because she wanted readers to respond emotionally to the struggles of her simple characters. Early in the book, she writes that black slaves "are not naturally daring and enterprising, but home-loving and affectionate." She aimed to make readers feel the suffering of slaves and develop compassion for gentle humans forced to live in inhumane conditions. Stowe compensated for the sentimental, depressing content of the book by sometimes using a humorous tone.

At the novel's close, George Shelby gives his slaves their freedom and promises to teach them how to use their new rights. Stowe hoped that southerners who read *Uncle Tom's Cabin* would be moved to do the same.

Religious Principles

Uncle Tom's Cabin was intended to make Americans reconsider the moral consequences of slavery. Stowe believed that more could be accomplished through faith in God than with change forced by military or political action.

This nineteenth-century engraving depicts the separation of a slave family after the sale of some of its members. The breakup of slave families was commonplace; Harriet Beecher Stowe found this particularly disturbing.

The Symbol of Uncle Tom's Cabin

The title of the book reveals one of Stowe's principal arguments against slavery. Uncle Tom's cabin itself represents domestic life, religious piety, and family love. When Tom is sold, the ideal family is torn apart. To Stowe, this is the most unforgivable sin of slavery.

Racial Stereotypes

A major challenge for Stowe was to convince a mostly white audience to sympathize with black characters. Stowe overcame this obstacle by using a number of techniques.

eminence; the Afric, born of ages of oppression, submission, ignorance, toil, and vice!

Topsy is portrayed as incapable of telling right from wrong. Ophelia, who believes slaves can be educated, cannot communicate well with Topsy. When Eva eventually develops a meaningful relationship with Topsy, Ophelia realizes that Topsy responds best to kindness. Through these characters, Stowe comments on the difficulty involved in educating children born into slavery. She also uses Topsy to demonstrate the positive effect of compassion on people who have been damaged by the abuse of slavery.

George and Eliza

Several characters, including Eliza and George Harris, are light-skinned blacks with some white blood. Stowe associates qualities of attractiveness, intelligence, and liveliness with people of mixed race. In a description of Eliza, she reflects on "that particular air of refinement, that softness of voice and manner, which seems in many cases to be a particular gift to the quadroon and mulatto women." She also refers to "natural graces," as a way to make these characters seem "less black" and easier to appreciate by her nineteenth-century white readers.

Mixed Racial Identity

Near the end of *Uncle Tom's Cabin*, George Harris experiences an inner conflict that Stowe presents as a struggle between the different desires of whites and blacks. His white urges, she tells us, are toward independence, power, and success, while his black urges are for service, spiritual strength, and a good work ethic. In reality, he struggles to balance the different expectations of whites and blacks in society.

The Unforgivable Sins of Slavery

Stowe called attention to the horrors of slavery, which she felt no Christian should overlook. Northerners did not escape criticism in the novel. Characters like Ophelia represent people in the North who opposed slavery on principle but did not show compassion in their actions. Stowe also condemned Christians who refused to educate blacks or welcome them into their churches.

Human Experiences

Perhaps Stowe's most effective technique was the way she used common human experiences to engage her readers' emotions. One theme that emerges in *Uncle Tom's Cabin* is the tragedy of losing a child. In Stowe's time, it was common for parents to lose one or more children to disease. Stowe's own son Samuel Charles died at the age of one in a cholera epidemic. Many women (and men) who read the book could relate to the intense fear and grief experienced by characters like Eliza.

Nearly all of the black female characters in *Uncle Tom's Cabin* live in fear of losing their children or have lost children. In addition to the danger of disease, there was the constant threat of a slaveholder selling away a slave's child. As Eliza sneaks off in the night with her son, Harry, Stowe asks the reader:

> **If it were your Harry, mother, or your Willie, that were going to be torn from you by a brutal trader, to-morrow morning . . . and you had only from twelve o'clock till morning to make good your escape . . . how fast could you walk?"**

Women Helping Women

Maternal instincts also create a bond between characters. Eliza finds a connection with Mrs. Bird when it is discovered that

Timeline

June 14, 1811

Harriet Beecher born to Lyman Beecher and Roxana Foote Beecher in Litchfield, Connecticut.

1817

The American Colonization Society is formed.

1823

Catharine Beecher founds Hartford Female Seminary. Harriet attends and begins teaching at age thirteen.

1833

Harriet visits a Kentucky plantation with her friend Mary Dutton. William Lloyd Garrison founds American Anti-Slavery Society.

both have endured the death of a child. Women at the Quaker settlement sympathize with Eliza's fierce protection of her son because love of their own children has taught them a great deal about Christian love.

Slave Marriages and Sexual Enslavement

Slave marriages were not protected by law, so husbands and wives were often separated, even when they had children together. Often a married slave would be sold to another household and be forced to have children with another slave.

Many slave women, especially those with partially white parentage, were sold for sexual purposes. Legree keeps two mistresses,

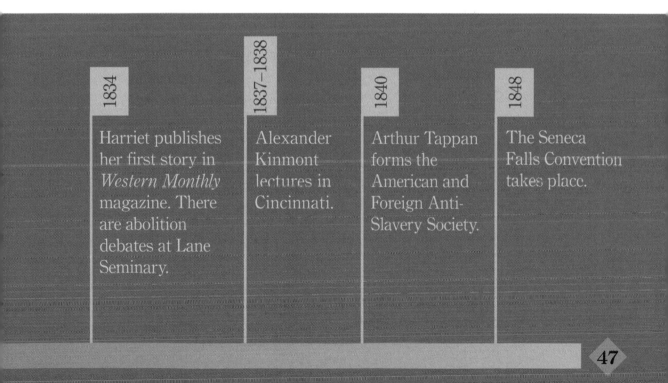

1834
Harriet publishes her first story in *Western Monthly* magazine. There are abolition debates at Lane Seminary.

1837–1838
Alexander Kinmont lectures in Cincinnati.

1840
Arthur Tappan forms the American and Foreign Anti-Slavery Society.

1848
The Seneca Falls Convention takes place.

Cassy and Emmeline. Stowe believed this was especially horrible because it forced the women to commit adultery.

Christian Values

In *Uncle Tom's Cabin*, Stowe reprimands Christians who do not live up to their own moral standards. Shortly after it was published, Stowe remarked, "The Lord himself wrote it, and I was but the humblest of instruments in His hand."

In the book, Senator and Mrs. Bird discuss the Fugitive Slave Act before Eliza appears at their door and asks for help.

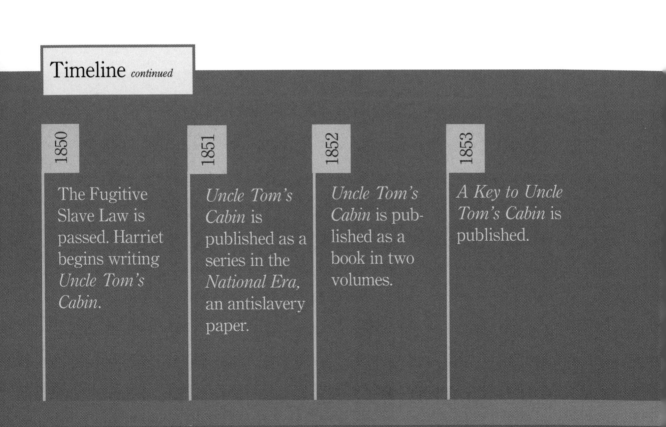

Timeline *continued*

1850

The Fugitive Slave Law is passed. Harriet begins writing *Uncle Tom's Cabin.*

1851

Uncle Tom's Cabin is published as a series in the *National Era,* an antislavery paper.

1852

Uncle Tom's Cabin is published as a book in two volumes.

1853

A Key to Uncle Tom's Cabin is published.

Mrs. Bird says to her husband, "I don't know anything about politics, but I can read my Bible and there I see that I must feed the hungry, clothe the naked, and comfort the desolate."

Tom symbolizes fundamental Christian values. It is often hard to tell if his admirable moral sense comes from his religion or his race. Stowe seems to think they go hand in hand. The reward that awaits him is salvation after death. This was the ultimate triumph as far as Stowe was concerned. The interactions between Eva and Tom emphasize the basic Christian values of love and compassion. When Eva dies, the people around her are profoundly affected by her example of goodness.

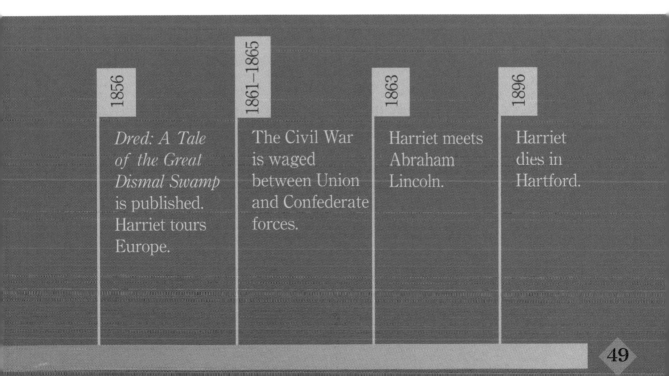

1856
Dred: A Tale of the Great Dismal Swamp is published. Harriet tours Europe.

1861–1865
The Civil War is waged between Union and Confederate forces.

1863
Harriet meets Abraham Lincoln.

1896
Harriet dies in Hartford.

The Good Wife

A recurring theme in *Uncle Tom's Cabin* is that of the good wife. Mrs. Shelby, Mrs. Bird, and Eliza all gently motivate their husbands to embrace what is decent and true. George Harris remarks, "I have an eloquent preacher of the Gospel ever by my side, in the person of my beautiful wife." This reflects Stowe's belief that women have a higher moral sense than men. It also reveals a lot about the place of women in nineteenth-century America and reinforces the idea that a woman's influence is primarily in the home.

Returning Slaves to Africa

Stowe hated slavery, but she did not support racial equality. She did not think blacks could fit into American culture. She wanted to educate free blacks and expose them to Christianity. But she thought they would ultimately be better off in Africa.

In *Uncle Tom's Cabin*, Stowe makes an argument for sending blacks to Africa primarily through the character of George Harris. Near the end of the novel, George, now living free in Canada, writes to a friend that he longs for a country of his own people. He writes

The desire and yearning of my soul is for an African nationality.

I want a people that shall have a tangible, separate existence of its own, and where am I to look for it? . . . On the shores of Africa I see a republic—a republic formed of picked men, who . . . raised themselves above a condition of slavery.

As she closes the novel, Stowe proclaims colonization as the best solution to slavery. She calls upon Christian men and women to pray for the "heathen at home" as well as those abroad. According to her, "the church of the north" should receive blacks into their churches and schools and give them a Christian education. Once they "have attained to somewhat of a moral and intellectual maturity," they should be sent to Africa to live the life for which they have been prepared. No other reforms appear as part of her plan.

Aside from African colonization, Stowe offers no original or realistic solution to slavery. Instead, she urges Americans—above all, Christians—to live by the principles they preach and set an example for the people around them. She claims that the country can only be saved by "repentance, justice and mercy." Without change, she warns, "injustice and cruelty shall bring on nations the wrath of Almighty God!" It almost sounds like she is predicting the end of the world or at least a great and violent catastrophe.

Chapter 6

The World Responds

Harriet Beecher Stowe met President Lincoln in 1853. As a legend recounts, Lincoln said, "So this is the little lady who made this big war." Whether he was serious, there was some truth in the comment. The reaction to *Uncle Tom's Cabin* was enormous. It intensified heated debate about slavery, which eventually led to the Civil War.

Stowe's Audience

Financially, *Uncle Tom's Cabin* was a surprising success. It became a best-seller in the United States and in parts of Europe and Asia. The first 5,000 copies sold in two days. By the end of the year, over 300,000 copies had been sold. The book was translated into thirty-seven languages and is estimated to have sold over two million copies in the United States and abroad.

Praise for *Uncle Tom's Cabin*

Established writers from all over the world praised Harriet Beecher Stowe for her work. Among them were Leo Tolstoy,

George Sand, Henry Wadsworth Longfellow, and Ralph Waldo Emerson. Over the next several years, Stowe toured Europe as a celebrated abolitionist writer. She met prominent political and literary figures and spoke to groups about the antislavery cause.

Shortly after the novel's publication, Charles W. Taylor wrote a stage version of *Uncle Tom's Cabin*, which was performed in front of large audiences for many years after.

Southerners Attack the Book

Not all of the response was positive. Stowe had expected people in the South to appreciate her portrayal of many slaveholders as honest and well intentioned. In her own voice, she addresses them as the "generous, noble-minded men and women, of the South—you, whose virtues, and magnanimity, and purity of character, are the greater for the severer trial it has encountered."

Instead, they found fault with her illustration of the South. Many southerners asserted that Stowe's depiction of slave conditions was inaccurate. Evidence today shows that her depictions were, in fact, quite realistic. Because Stowe never encountered field slaves, most of the slave characters in *Uncle Tom's Cabin* work in the house. House slaves were considered more privileged than those who worked in the field. They were sometimes educated while field slaves were not. In this way, her representation may have been unbalanced.

Abolitionists Angered

The book even angered some abolitionists because Stowe recommends sending freed blacks to Africa. Freed blacks in the North were upset by this idea because they had worked very hard to secure their rights and live as Americans.

To reinforce her position, Stowe chose a slave character, George Harris, as the spokesperson for colonization. "Our nation," says George, "shall roll the tide of civilization and Christianity along its shores, and plant there mighty republics." This was quite an optimistic outlook. By the time the book was written, the idea of colonization was past its prime. The attempt to start the colony of Liberia in Africa had failed for the most part. Abolitionists wished that Stowe had supported outlawing slavery instead of reverting to colonization.

Abolitionists also took issue with Stowe's implication that slaves in Kentucky were better cared for than slaves in the Deep South. Abolitionists did not think better treatment excused the use of slavery.

 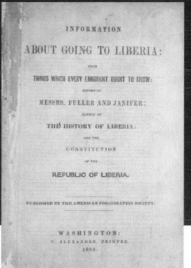

At left, a portrait of Joseph Jenkins Roberts, who became president of Liberia in 1848; at right, an American Colonization Society pamphlet, circa 1840, providing tips about moving to and living in Liberia.

However, even those abolitionists who did not agree with Stowe on every issue appreciated that she had written *Uncle Tom's Cabin*. It was a brave objection to the institution of slavery and a clear challenge to those who upheld it.

Conflict Escalates Toward Civil War

When Lincoln became president in 1860, his challenge was to keep the Union together, with or without slavery. But before he was even sworn into office, South Carolina seceded from the Union. By January 1861, Alabama, Arkansas, Florida, Georgia,

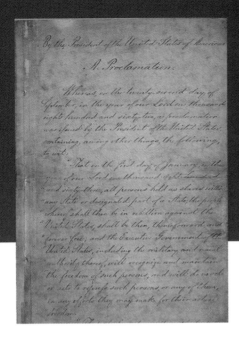

In the Emancipation Proclamation of 1863 *(left)*, President Abraham Lincoln decreed that all slaves who lived in the Confederate states were from then on "forever free." Harriet Beecher Stowe's meeting with Lincoln—in which he referred to her as "the little lady who made this big war"—is captured in this painting *(right)* by Harry Everett Townsend.

Louisiana, Mississippi, North Carolina, Tennessee, Texas, and Virginia had also left the Union. Within a month, they formed the Confederate States of America. On April 12, 1861, Confederate soldiers attacked Union soldiers at Fort Sumter, South Carolina. Thus began the Civil War.

The Emancipation Proclamation

In January 1863, Lincoln signed the Emancipation Proclamation, which freed slaves in the Confederate states. Large numbers of slaves began to escape, and the foundation of slavery slowly crumbled. In 1865, the Thirteenth Amendment to the Constitution made slavery illegal everywhere in the United States.

Stowe did not stop writing after she finished *Uncle Tom's Cabin*. *A Key to Uncle Tom's Cabin*, published the following year, in 1853, dealt with her critics' arguments point by point. In it, she presented documentation to further establish the "truth" of her book. In 1856, she published another antislavery novel, entitled *Dred: A Tale of the Great Dismal Swamp*. This novel was not as well written as *Uncle Tom's Cabin* and never became popular to readers. In later novels and articles, Stowe mainly addressed religion.

The Long-Range Influences of *Uncle Tom's Cabin*

Uncle Tom's Cabin not only shaped the political and social sphere in which it was written, but it also changed activism for generations to come. Harriet Beecher Stowe set an example for other women who wished to voice their opinions, even if they weren't made to feel welcome in politics. Her courage reassured others of the importance of defending their principles. She helped to establish a place for writers in social reform. The phenomenal influence of *Uncle Tom's Cabin* does not demonstrate the strength of Stowe's ideas so much as it testifies to the promise her novel made: that an individual, with imagination and resolve, can inspire a nation to reconsider its most basic ideals.

Glossary

abolitionist   A member of the movement to abolish, or completely eliminate, slavery.

advocate   A person who speaks or writes in support of a cause.

ancestry   The relatives from whom a person is descended; ancestors.

cholera   A dangerous and contagious bacterial disease transmitted through infected food and water. Symptoms include diarrhea, extreme dehydration, and weakness, and the disease often ends in death.

conversion   A religious experience that results in a more passionate observation of the beliefs of a particular religion.

epidemic   The sudden widespread occurrence of a disease in a particular place and time.

fugitive   Someone fleeing persecution, consequences of the law, or dangerous conditions.

Fugitive Slave Act of 1850   Part of a law passed in 1850 that provided penalties for U.S. citizens, including those in free states, who assisted escaped slaves or did not return a wanted fugitive to his or her owners.

innate   Natural, present from birth, or not a product of experience.

monogenesis   The theory that all organisms evolved from one original organism or that all races evolved from one original race.

mulatto   A person with one white parent and one black parent.

parentage   Parents, or ancestry slightly farther down the family line. Descent from one's parents and ancestors.

polygenesis   The theory that human races originated from several different races that all began around the same time.

propaganda   Informational materials and ideas that are distributed with the intent to influence people's opinion about a subject.

prototype   An original model from which copies are made.

quadroon   A person who is one-quarter black and three-quarters white; an offensive term.

seminary   An educational institution, often with a religious affiliation.

slave trader   Someone in charge of buying slaves and transporting them to an auction or to a new household.

stereotype   A statement of observation, often damaging, that is broadly applied to an entire group of people.

suffrage   The right to vote.

theology   The study of God and related subjects, such as religion and morality; a particular system of religious teaching and practice.

For More Information

Harriet Beecher Stowe Center
77 Forest Street
Hartford, CT 06105
(860) 522-9258
Web site: http://www.harrietbeecherstowecenter.org

Web Sites

Due to the changing nature of Internet links, the Rosen Publishing Group, Inc., has developed an online list of Web sites related to the subject of this book. This site is updated regularly. Please use this link to access the list:

http://www.rosenlinks.com/lal/untc

For Further Reading

Fritz, Jean. *Harriet Beecher Stowe and the Beecher Preachers.* New York: G. P. Putnam's Sons, 1994.

Henson, Josiah. *The Life of Josiah Henson: Formerly a Slave, Now an Inhabitant of Canada, as Narrated By Himself.* Bedford, MA: Applewood Books, 2003.

Stowe, Harriet Beecher. *The Key to Uncle Tom's Cabin.* New York: Arno Press, 1968.

Bibliography

Ammons, Elizabeth, and Susan Belasco. *Approaches to Teaching Stowe's Uncle Tom's Cabin*. New York: The Modern Language Association of America, 2000.

Donovan, Josephine. *Uncle Tom's Cabin: Evil, Affliction, and Redemptive Love*. Boston: Twayne Publishers, 1991.

Furnas, J. C. *Goodbye to Uncle Tom*. New York: Apollo Editions, 1956.

Gossett, Thomas F. *Uncle Tom's Cabin and American Culture*. Dallas: Southern Methodist University Press, 1985.

Hedrick, Joan D. *Harriet Beecher Stowe: A Life*. New York: Oxford University Press, 1995.

Kirkham, E. Bruce. *The Building of Uncle Tom's Cabin*. Knoxville, TN: University of Tennessee Press, 1977.

Stowe, Harriet Beecher. *Uncle Tom's Cabin*. Elizabeth Ammons, ed. New York: W. W. Norton and Company, 1994.

Sundquist, Eric J., ed. *New Essays on Uncle Tom's Cabin*. Cambridge, England: Cambridge University Press, 1987.

Wagenknecht, Edward. *Harriet Beecher Stowe: The Known and the Unknown*. New York: Oxford University Press, 1965.

Walters, Ronald G. *The Anti-Slavery Appeal: American Abolitionism After 1830*. Baltimore: John Hopkins University Press, 1976.

Yellin, Jean Fagan, and John C. Van Horne, eds. *The Abolitionist Sisterhood: Women's Political Culture in Antebellum America*. Ithaca, NY: Cornell University Press, 1994.

Primary Source Image List

Cover (top): Portrait of Harriet Beecher Stowe, 1853. Oil on canvas. Housed at the National Portrait Gallery, Smithsonian Institution, in Washington, D.C.

Cover (bottom left): Broadside featuring woodcut image of a slave in chains, 1837. Housed at the Rare Books and Special Collections Division at the Library of Congress in Washington, D.C.

Cover (bottom right): Cover of first edition of *Uncle Tom's Cabin,* published in 1852. Part of the Barrett Collection at the University of Virginia.

Page 5: Title page of first edition of *Uncle Tom's Cabin; or, Life Among the Lowly,* as published in 1852. Housed in the Library of American History Special Collections Department at the University of Virginia in Charlottesville, Virginia.

Page 7 (bottom): Portrait of Isaac Jefferson, daguerreotype created in 1845. Housed in the Library of American History, Special Collections Department at the University of Virginia in Charlottesville, Virginia.

Page 10: Title page of Alexander Kinmont's *Twelve Lectures on the Natural History of Man, and the Rise and Progress of Philosophy.* Published in 1839. Housed at the New York Public Library.

Page 16: Broadside entitled "The Fugitive Slave Law" by S. M. Africanus. Printed in Hartford, Connecticut, in 1850. It is housed in the Rare Books and Special Collections Division in the Library of Congress.

Page 19: Front page of the *Liberator* newspaper, January 1, 1831. Housed in the Rare Books and Special Collections Division of the Library of Congress in Washington, D.C.

Page 19 (inset): Portrait of William Lloyd Garrison as published in *Underground Railroad* by William Still, 1879. Housed in the Rare Books and Special Collections Division of the Library of Congress in Washington, D.C.

Page 21: American Anti-Slavery Society broadside, published in 1840. Housed in the Rare Books and Special Collections Division of the Library of Congress in Washington, D.C.

Page 23: June 20, 1850, edition of the *North Star,* an abolitionist newspaper that Frederick Douglass published. Housed in the Rare Books and Special Collections Division of the Library of Congress in Washington, D.C.

Page 23 (inset): Portrait of Frederick Douglass, housed at the Library of Congress in Washington, D.C.

Page 25: Photograph of Harriet Beecher Stowe with her father and most of her siblings, 1855.

Page 27: Etching of the Hartford Female Seminary, 1862. Housed at the Harriet Beecher Stowe Center in Hartford, Connecticut.

Page 28: Photograph of Harriet Beecher Stowe and Calvin Stowe, taken around 1850 by George K. Warren. Housed at The Arthur and Elizabeth Schesinger Library on the History of Women in America at Harvard University.

Page 30: Title pages from *The May Flower and Miscellaneous Writings* by Harriet Beecher Stowe. Published in 1855. Housed at the New York Public Library.

Page 33: The first page of the June 2, 1851, edition of the *National Era,* bearing chapter 1 of *Uncle Tom's Cabin.*

Page 39 (left): Illustrated page from *Uncle Tom's Cabin,* 1852. Housed at the New York Public Library.

Page 39 (right): Portrait of Josiah Henson as it appeared on the frontispiece of his 1858 autobiography, *Truth Stranger Than Fiction: Father Henson's Story of His Own Life.* Housed at the Schomburg Center of the New York Public Library.

Page 41: *The Separation of a Family of Slaves After Being Seized and Sold Upon a Warrant of Destraint for Their Master's Debts,* engraving, circa 1800. Part of a private collection.

Page 43: An illustration from the 1853 London edition of *Uncle Tom's Cabin.* Housed at the New York Public Library.

Page 53: Poster ad for *Uncle Tom's Cabin,* 1859.

Page 55 (left): Portrait of Joseph Jenkins Roberts, circa 1855. Housed in the Prints and Photographs Division of the Library of Congress in Washington, D.C.

Page 55 (right): American Colonization Society pamphlet, circa 1840. Housed in the Manuscript Division of the Library of Congress in Washington, D.C.

Page 56 (left): The Emancipation Proclamation, signed by Abraham Lincoln on January 1, 1863. Housed at the U.S. National Archives and Records Administration in Washington, D.C.

Page 56 (right): *Abraham Lincoln with Harriet Beecher Stowe* by Harry Everett Townsend, charcoal on paper. Housed at the New Britain Museum of American Art in Connecticut.

Index

About the Author

Julie Carlson is a writer who lives in Oberlin, Ohio.

Photo Credits

Cover (top), pp. 25, 27 courtesy of the Harriet Beecher Stowe Center, Hartford, Connecticut; cover (bottom right), pp. 16, 19, 21 Library of Congress, Rare Books and Special Collections Division; cover (bottom left), pp. 5, 7 (bottom) Special Collections, University of Virginia Library; pp. 7 (top), 12 © Hulton/Archive/Getty Images; pp. 10, 30 General Research Division, New York Public Library Astor, Lenox, and Tilden Foundations; p. 15 http://teachpol.tcnj.edu; p. 23 Library of Congress Serial and Government Publications Division; pp. 23 (inset), 55 (left) Library of Congress Prints and Photographs Division; p. 28 The Schlesinger Library, Radcliffe Institute, Harvard University; p. 37 Art Resource, NY; pp. 39 (left), 43 Print Collection, Miriam and Ira D. Wallach Division of Art, Prints, and Photographs, New York Public Library Astor, Lenox, and Tilden Foundations; p. 39 (right) Documenting the American South (http://docsouth.unc.edu), The University of North Carolina at Chapel Hill Libraries; p. 41 private collection/ Bridgeman Art Library; p. 42 © Myron H. Kimball/Gilman Paper Company Collection; p. 53 © Bettmann/Corbis; p. 55 (right) courtesy of the New York Public Library Schomburg Center; p. 56 (left) Record Group 11, Old Military and Civil Records, National Archives and Records Administration; p. 56 (right) New Britain Museum of American Art, Connecticut, Gift of James H. Dougherty.

Design: Les Kanturek; Editor: Jill Jarnow; Photo Researcher: Rebecca Anguin-Cohen